STEP-BY-STEP
50 Great Sandwiches

STEP-BY-STEP

50 Great Sandwiches

Carole Handslip

Photography by Edward Allwright

SMITHMARK

This edition published in 1994 by
SMITHMARK Publishers Inc.
16 East 32nd Street
New York
NY 10016

SMITHMARK books are available for bulk purchase for sales
promotion and for premium use. For details write or call
the manager of special sales, SMITHMARK Publishers Inc.
16 East 32nd Street, New York, 10016; (212) 532–6600

ISBN 0 8317 6517 8

Produced by Anness Publishing Limited
1 Boundary Row
London SE1 8HP

Printed and bound in Italy by Graphicom S.r.l., Vicenza

CONTENTS

INTRODUCTION

The sandwich is said to have been originated in England by the Earl of that name. The fourth Earl of Sandwich (1718–92) was a keen gambler, and so as not to waste time eating away from the gaming tables, he asked to have cold beef placed between two slices of bread in order to continue playing while eating. This very convenient manner of taking sustaining nourishment quickly became popular, and in deference to its inventor became known as the 'sandwich'.

Though the basic idea has remained the same for more than two hundred years, there are now many permutations. The variety and availability of different and excellent breads is enormous, and ideas for fillings abound throughout the world. Each country has its own particular way of preparing this quick and easy snack. In Spain they make *bocadillas*, long rolls stuffed with Serrano ham. In Italy *bruschetta* is a toasted, peasant bread lavishly spread with garlic, olive oil and sometimes tomato. In northern Europe, Germany offers black or rye breads with smoky Westphalia ham. Scandinavia uses pumpernickel with many varieties of herring. From America we have triple-decker club sandwiches and torpedo rolls filled to bursting, called 'heroes', designed to satisfy an heroic appetite! From the East come tikka, satay and other hot, spicy goodies which can be stuffed into pita bread or simply wrapped in naan – the variety is endless.

In this book are recipes ideal to pack for picnics or to make a lunch box more interesting; there are some great surprises for a children's party; and other recipes will provide inviting, tasty food for the unexpected visitor. When it's just too late to prepare a full cooked meal, a piece of bread with butter and a little of what you fancy will provide a noble supper crust.

Seasonings

Sandwiches are essentially quick and easy, and are often presented as a meal; it is therefore sensible to maintain a well-stocked pantry and refrigerator so that you can rustle up a satisfying snack at a moment's notice. Ingredients like as tuna fish, anchovies, olives, pickled herrings, good olive oil, a jar of pesto, mayonnaise, sun-dried tomatoes, and olive paste will enable you to provide a feast, as long as you have some good bread to fill. Remember: you don't have to stick to any particular filling for a certain bread – chop and change to suit your appetite, or what you have available. Once opened, most bottled sauces should be stored in the refrigerator, where they will keep for about 1 month, but read the labels carefully for advice. Prepared mustards can be kept in the pantry, but not for too long, as they begin to dry out and darken after a few months.

Dill mustard sauce
This is a sweetened mustard sauce flavored with dill. It is excellent mixed with a little sour cream and served with gravlax.

Extra-virgin olive oil
This oil is used for flavor in marinades and dressings, and as a dip for bread.

Jalapeño peppers
In their pickled form, these hot green chilies are ideal for adding zip to fillings, from the traditional Mexican taco to a simple cheese sandwich.

Mustards
Mustards are made from black, brown, or white mustard seeds that are ground and then mixed with spices and, usually, wine vinegar. There are many flavored mustards available, including horseradish, honey, chili, and tarragon. Meaux mustard is made from mixed mustard seed, and has a grainy texture with a warm, spicy flavor. Dijon mustard is medium-hot with a sharp taste, and is ideal in dressings. German mustard has a sweet-sour flavor, and is best with frankfurters.

Olive paste
This is made with puréed black or green olives, olive oil, and herbs. Delicious on its own, spread on some good bread, it is also very useful for spreading on bread before covering with topping and broiling, and for adding to sauces.

Pesto
This is a rich, pungent sauce made with basil, Parmesan cheese, pine nuts, and garlic.

Red pesto
This is similar to pesto, but with the addition of sun-dried tomatoes.

Sauerkraut
This salted and fermented white cabbage, often spiced as well, is a useful accompaniment to sausages. It is good mixed with tomato mayonnaise and used in sandwiches.

Sun-dried tomatoes
These are preserved whole by drying and have a dense texture and highly concentrated flavor. You can also buy them chopped and mixed with olive oil and herbs. Delicious used as a spread, or in sauces.

whole-grain mustard

dill mustard sauce

crushed sun-dried tomatoes

Dijon mustard

sun-dried tomatoes

German mustard

olive oil

chopped chili

black olive paste

concentrated curry sauce

pesto

green olive paste

red pesto

Jalapeño peppers

sauerkraut

chicory

cilantro

mint

dill

thyme

chives

nasturtium

fennel

violet

arugula

basil

flat-leaf parsley

Herbs and Flowers

Fresh herbs have been used liberally in the recipes in this book, for they give terrific zip to a sandwich filling. They can easily be grown, either in the garden or on a windowsill, and have so much more flavor when they are freshly picked.

Flowers make a delightful garnish, are very pretty to look at and have a sweet taste. Marigolds, pansies, violas, and violets can all be used, as can many of the herb flowers such as borage, thyme, marjoram, mint, and rosemary – they all add color and flavor.

Basil
Basil has a warm, spicy scent and pungent flavor. It is wonderful with tomatoes, and is good used either cooked in a sauce or as fresh whole leaves added to a sandwich filling.

Chives
Chives give a delicate, mild, onion flavor to sauces and fillings. The slender leaves make attractive garnishes, and the beautiful purple flowers can also be eaten.

Chicory
Chicory leaves can be eaten fresh when young. The flowers make attractive garnishes.

Cilantro
Cilantro is an intensely aromatic herb with a spicy flavor; an essential ingredient in Indian, Chinese, and Mexican dishes.

Fennel and Dill
These herbs are both from the same family, with similar feathery leaves, but fennel has a more pronounced aniseed flavor. They are particularly good with fish.

Marjoram and Oregano
These herbs belong to the same family and have similar uses, but oregano is slightly stronger. They are good in tomato sauces and egg dishes. The flowers make a pretty garnish.

Mint
Mint is used mainly as a garnish, but can also be mixed with soft cheeses or added to broiled meats for a Middle Eastern flavor.

Nasturtium
Nasturtium flowers are edible and make a stunning addition to sandwiches. The leaves have a peppery flavor.

Parsley
Curly and flat-leaf parsley are both available, the latter having a stronger flavor. Apart from being an attractive garnish, parsley is also excellent chopped and added to an herb butter.

Thyme
Thyme should be used in cooked dishes for the best flavor.

Breads

There are many interesting types of bread available now — different sizes, shapes, textures, flavors, even colors — making it possible for the sandwich enthusiast to be much more adventurous and to produce some exciting and very tasty creations. Do make the most of the wide variety on offer.

Bagel
Bagels are best served warm, and are especially good when filled with cream cheese and smoked salmon or other smoked fish.

Brioche
This light, rich, slightly sweet bread makes a good base for open sandwiches when toasted.

Baguette
Baguettes, or French bread, can be split lengthways, broiled and cut into lengths to suit the appetite.

Ciabatta
Ciabatta is made with olive oil and has a light texture. It is available plain or flavored.

Country bread
A crusty white loaf, suitable for hearty and toasted sandwiches.

Croissant
Croissants are delicious with both sweet and savory fillings. Warm them first, then split and fill.

Flavored breads
These might include multi-grain, onion bread, and cheese and herb bread. They all make excellent vehicles for many fillings.

Pita bread
These are available in both whole-wheat and white, in rounds, ovals and mini cocktail shapes. They are ideal for filling with broiled meats and salads.

Pugliese
This is also known as Italian peasant bread, and is a close-textured loaf made with olive oil.

Pumpernickel
This is a heavy, close-textured black rye bread with a distinctive flavor. It is excellent as a base for open sandwiches, topped with strongly flavored foods.

Rye bread
Both light and dark rye breads are available and some varieties are seeded. Rye bread is delicious with pickled herring.

Sourdough bread
This speciality from San Francisco is now known the world over. It has a distinctive sharp flavor, ideal for many fillings, and comes in loaves, baguettes, and rolls.

Tortilla
This traditional Mexican pancake comes in both corn and flour varieties. Always warm first before serving with a savory filling.

White bread
White bread need not be the pre-packaged, pre-sliced variety. Bakeries will make their own varieties, which have a lot more flavor and a better texture.

Whole-wheat bread
Whole-wheat bread is preferred by some to white bread for its added flavor and texture.

croissants

pugliese (Italian peasant bread)

bagels

pumpernickel

ciabatta rolls

ciabatta

baguette

brioche

pita bread

rye breads

half-baguette

wheat tortillas

multi-grain

sourdough bread

corn tortillas

white loaf

whole-wheat bread

country bread

Cheese-Tomato Baguette

A wholesome multi-grain bread with the addition of
tomato and Parmesan cheese.

Makes 2 sticks

INGREDIENTS
2 cups whole-wheat flour
2 cups all-purpose flour
1 tsp salt
1 tsp dried yeast
1¼ cups warm water
pinch of sugar
2 tbsp tomato paste or sun-dried
  tomato paste
¼ cup grated Parmesan cheese
4 scallions, chopped
cracked wheat or sesame seeds

1 Mix the flours and salt in a bowl. Put the yeast in a small bowl and mix in half the water and a pinch of sugar to help activate the yeast. Leave for 10 minutes until dissolved, then add to the flour.

2 Add the tomato paste, cheese, scallions, and remaining water. Mix to a soft dough, adding a little more water if necessary.

3 Transfer to a floured surface and knead for 5 minutes until the dough is smooth and elastic.

4 Place in a mixing bowl, cover with a damp cloth, and leave in a warm place to rise until doubled in size.

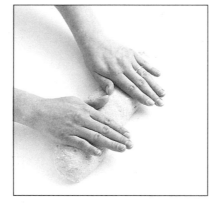

5 Transfer to a floured surface and knead again for a few minutes. Divide the dough in half, shape each portion into a loaf 12 in long, and place diagonally on a greased baking sheet.

6 Make diagonal cuts down the length of the loaves, brush with water, and sprinkle with cracked wheat or sesame seeds. Cover and leave in a warm place to rise for about 30 minutes until doubled in size. Preheat the oven to 425°F. Bake the bread in the oven for 10 minutes, then lower the temperature to 400°F and bake for 15 minutes more.

CHEESE-TOMATO ROLLS
Divide the dough into 8 portions and shape into rolls. Bake for 20–25 minutes.

Filling Ingredients

Avocado
Avocado imparts a subtle flavor to sandwiches, and mixes well with brie or shrimp.

Bell Peppers
These make a crunchy and flavorful addition to fillings.

Blue cheese
This cheese combines particularly well with pears or other fruit.

Brie
Brie should be soft in the center when used. It is delicious with avocado and tomato.

Capers
The piquant flavor of capers is useful in dressings.

Cucumber
Remove the skin to make these more digestible.

Eggs
Very versatile; use in almost any form with a variety of toppings.

Lemon
Lemon is a tasty addition to fish fillings.

Lettuce
There are so many different varieties available it is worth experimenting with different combinations.

Mozzarella
Mozzarella is another good melting cheese that blends well with sun-dried tomato and olive paste.

Olives
These are a particularly good addition to toasted toppings.

Parmesan
Use freshly grated Parmesan for more flavor.

Pastrami
Pastrami is cured brisket of beef, which is then smoked. It is best served with a strong-flavored bread such as rye.

Pickled herrings
Pickled herring are excellent for open-faced sandwiches.

Prosciutto
This is cured, matured ham, which is sliced very thinly. It is suitable for delicate party sandwiches.

Quails' eggs
A luxurious addition to open sandwiches. Boil for 5 minutes, plunge into cold water, and peel.

Salami
There is a huge range of salamis available, both smoked and unsmoked.

Shrimp
For the best flavor, use North Atlantic shrimp.

Smoked salmon
This is ideal for open sandwiches and pinwheels, and can be chopped and served in croissants.

Swiss cheese
This is the classic cheese for melting under the broiler.

Tomatoes
Again, these come in so many different varieties that it is worth experimenting. Make sure they are deep red for the best flavor.

blue cheese

Swiss cheese

Brie

mozzarella

Parmesan

pickled herring

shrimp

smoked salmon

pastrami

lemon

tomatoes

avocado

cucumber

salami

quails' eggs

eggs

bell peppers

lollo rosso lettuce

prosciutto

capers

olives

frisée lettuce

Mayonnaise

Homemade mayonnaise contains raw egg yolks – always use a reputable supplier to ensure the eggs are fresh. Raw eggs are not suitable for young children, expectant mothers, and the elderly. Mayonnaise can be made by hand, or prepared in a food processor or blender – whizz 1 whole egg together with the seasonings and vinegar, then gradually add the oil in a thin stream. Store in an airtight container in the refrigerator for up to 2 weeks.

Makes about 1 ¹/₂ cups

INGREDIENTS
2 egg yolks
salt and pepper
¹/₂ tsp Dijon mustard
1 ¹/₄ cups sunflower oil
2 tsp wine vinegar

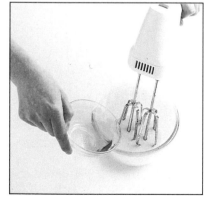

1 Beat the egg yolk, seasoning, and mustard together in a bowl with a hand whisk. Add the oil drop by drop, whisking vigorously.

2 As the mixture thickens, add the vinegar, then continue to add the remaining oil in a steady stream, whisking all the time. Add a little boiling water to thin if necessary.

Gravlax Sauce

This is used with gravlax, Scandinavian marinated salmon, but its piquant flavor goes well with beef too. It will keep for up to 2 weeks in a sealed container in the refrigerator.

Makes about ²/₃ cup

INGREDIENTS
2 tbsp German mustard
1 tsp superfine sugar
1 tsp wine vinegar
2 tbsp oil
2 tbsp sour cream
1 tbsp chopped fresh dill

1 Beat the mustard, sugar, and vinegar together. Gradually add the oil, beating well between each addition.

2 Mix in the cream and dill.

Peanut Sauce

This peanut sauce is traditionally served with Indonesian satay. It is good with chicken, duck, pork, and any vegetable filling, and is also delicious used as a dip. It keeps for up to 1 week in the refrigerator.

Makes about 1¹⁄₄ cups

INGREDIENTS
1 tbsp sunflower oil
1 small onion, chopped
1 garlic clove, crushed
1 tsp ground cumin
1 tsp ground coriander
¹⁄₂ tsp chili powder
3 tbsp crunchy peanut butter
2 tsp soy sauce
1 tsp lemon juice

1 Heat the oil in a pan and fry the onion until softened. Add the garlic and spices and fry for 1 minute more, stirring. Mix in the peanut butter and blend in ²⁄₃ cup water. Bring to a boil, stirring, then cover and cook for 5 minutes.

2 Transfer to a bowl and stir in the soy sauce and lemon juice. Thin with a little more water if liked. Allow to cool.

Fennel and Sour Cream Dressing

A light, creamy dressing to use with seafood or cucumber fillings. You can make a green herb sauce by adding 3 tbsp chopped fresh parsley, chives, and mint. It keeps for up to 1 week in the refrigerator.

Makes about ²⁄₃ cup

INGREDIENTS
¹⁄₂ cup thick sour cream
2 tsp lemon juice
1 garlic clove, crushed
1 tsp clear honey
2 tbsp chopped fresh fennel
salt and pepper

1 Put the sour cream into a bowl, add the lemon juice, garlic, and honey and mix thoroughly.

2 Add the fennel and some salt and pepper, and stir to blend.

Equipment

Very little special equipment is needed for sandwich making, apart from a good bread knife so that you can slice bread evenly and cut sandwiches into portions. Hot sandwich makers, although useful, are by no means essential for making toasted or fried sandwiches – a skillet or griddle does just as well. However, if you want to make sandwiches for special occasions, or add a little extra flair with garnishes, the following pieces of equipment may be useful to have on hand.

Bread knife
A good-quality bread knife will ensure bread is cut evenly.

Cheese grater
This is invaluable for preparing fillings, both for grating hard cheeses and vegetables.

Cutters
Both plain and shaped cutters are useful for making party sandwiches and canapés. Novelty cutters are especially appealing to children.

Knives
Keep knives clean and well sharpened.

Measuring cups
When using measuring cups and spoons make sure you level the top of the utensil, unless otherwise stated.

Measuring spoons
Accurate measuring spoons are essential to successful baking.

Metal spatula
Metal spatulas are useful for spreading fillings smoothly.

Mixing bowls
A set of mixing bowls of various sizes is invaluable. Keep large bowls on hand for making bread (to allow the dough to rise).

Pastry brush
A pastry brush is useful both for bread and sandwich making. Use for egg glazes on uncooked bread dough, and for brushing bread with melted butter or oils.

Rolling pin
When making sandwiches such as Asparagus Rolls, flatten slices of bread with a heavy rolling pin, so that the slices roll up more easily.

Saucepan
A heavy metal saucepan should be used for melted and cooked fillings.

Spatula
Use a flexible rubber spatula for spreading and transferring fillings from mixing bowls.

Spoons, metal
Ordinary soup and dessert spoons may be used for mixing ingredients.

Spoons, wooden
Wooden spoons may be used for mixing both hot and cold fillings.

Wire whisk
Use a wire whisk for mixing hot fillings and sauces.

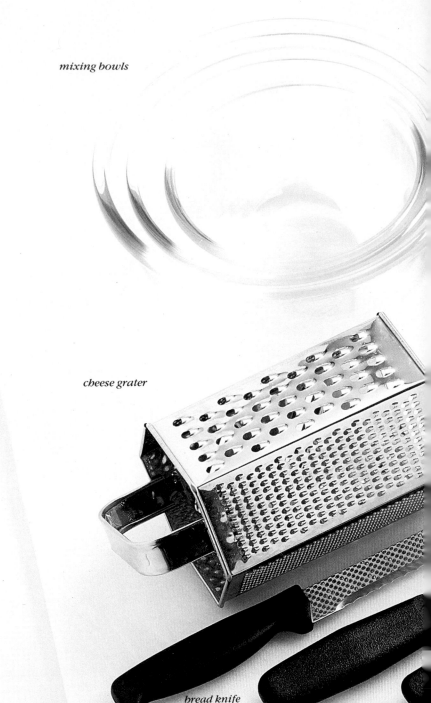

mixing bowls

cheese grater

bread knife

metal spatulas

wire whisk

metal spoons

saucepan

cutters

astry brush

wooden spoon

measuring jug

rolling pin

knives

measuring spoons

spatula

Avocado Filling

This filling is particularly suitable for sandwich horns, croissants or on open sandwiches.

INGREDIENTS
1 avocado, pitted and chopped
1 scallion, chopped
2 tsp lemon juice
dash Worcestershire sauce
salt and pepper

1 Put the avocado pieces in a blender, or mash with a fork until smooth. Mix in the chopped scallion, lemon juice, and seasonings and blend well.

Tuna and Tomato Filling

This recipe is sufficient to fill 3 sandwiches.

INGREDIENTS
3 oz can tuna fish, drained
2 tbsp softened butter or margarine
1 tbsp tomato ketchup
1 tbsp mayonnaise
salt and pepper

1 Put the tuna fish in a bowl and flake with a fork. Add the butter or margarine, tomato ketchup, and mayonnaise and season to taste. Mix well until blended.

Egg and Sprout Filling

This recipe is sufficient to fill 3 sandwiches.

INGREDIENTS
2 hard-cooked eggs, shelled and finely chopped
¼ cup smooth cottage cheese
2 tbsp mayonnaise
salt and pepper
1 packet small fresh sprouts

1 Mix the ingredients together in a bowl until thoroughly combined and smooth.

Garnishes

The presentation of food is almost as important as the taste. The first contact is by sight, and if the food offered appears attractive and appetizing, the taste-buds go into action creating the desire to eat.

These suggestions are for garnishes that not only look good, but also add their own flavor.

Carrot curl

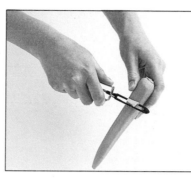

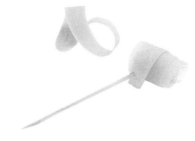

Using a vegetable peeler, remove thin strips of carrot. Roll each strip to make a curl and secure with a toothpick. Place in ice water for about 1 hour to keep the shape.

Scallion tassel

Trim a scallion to about 3 in long. Cut lengthwise through the green part of the scallion several times, to within 1½ in of the white end. Place in a bowl of ice water for about 1 hour, until the green ends curl up.

Radish chrysanthemum

First remove the stalk, then cut downwards across the radish, using a sharp knife, at ¹⁄₁₆ in intervals, keeping the radish joined at the base. Then cut in the opposite direction to form minute squares. Drop into ice water for about 1 hour, until it opens out like a flower.

Tomato rose

Choose a firm tomato and, starting at the smooth end, pare off the skin in a continuous strip about ½ in wide using a sharp knife. With the flesh side inwards, start to curl the strip of skin from the base end, forming a bud shape. Continue winding the strip into a flower.

Radish rose

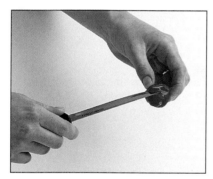

Remove the stalk, and with the pointed end of a vegetable knife cut petal shapes around the bottom half of the radish, keeping them joined at the base. Cut a second row of petals in between and above the first row, and continue in this way until you reach the top of the radish. Leave in ice water for about 1 hour until it opens.

Cucumber butterflies

Cut a ½ in length of cucumber and halve lengthwise into 2 semi-circles. Cut each into 7 slices, leaving them attached along one edge. Fold every other slice back on itself to form the butterfly.

Filled Croissants

Croissants are very versatile and can be used with sweet or savory fillings.

Makes 2

INGREDIENTS
2 croissants
knob of butter
2 eggs
salt and pepper
1 tablespoon heavy cream
2 oz smoked salmon, chopped
1 sprig fresh dill, to garnish

croissants

smoked salmon

eggs

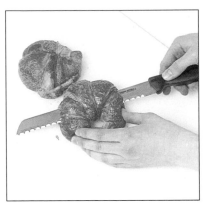

1 Preheat the oven to 350°F. Slice the croissants in half horizontally and warm in the oven for 5–6 minutes.

2 Melt a knob of butter in a small pan. Beat the eggs in a bowl with seasoning to taste.

3 Add the eggs to the pan and cook for 2 minutes, stirring constantly.

4 Remove from the heat and stir in the cream and smoked salmon.

5 Spoon the smoked salmon mixture into the warmed croissants and garnish.

PEAR AND STILTON FILLING

Soften 4 oz Stilton cheese with a fork and mix in 1 peeled, cored, and chopped ripe pear and 1 tbsp chopped chives with a little black pepper. Spoon into a split croissant and bake in a preheated oven for 5 minutes.

Crispy Hot Dogs

Crisp little envelopes enclose succulent frankfurters —
use broiled French-style sausages if you prefer and
vary the flavoring with different sauces.

Makes 8

INGREDIENTS
8 slices white or brown bread, crusts
   removed
4 tbsp soft margarine
1 tbsp German mustard
8 frankfurters
sauerkraut, to serve
tomato wedges and flat-leaf parsley,
   to garnish

white bread

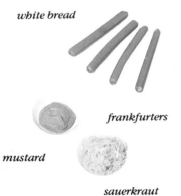

frankfurters

mustard

sauerkraut

1 Preheat the oven to 400°F. Roll the
bread lightly with a rolling pin so that it
rolls up more easily.

2 Spread the bread with a little
margarine and mustard.

3 Place a frankfurter diagonally across
each slice of bread and roll up tightly,
securing with a toothpick. Spread each
roll with margarine and place on a baking
sheet. Bake in the oven for 15–20
minutes until golden. Meanwhile, heat the
sauerkraut. Remove the toothpicks from
the hot dogs and serve with hot
sauerkraut and a garnish of tomato
wedges and flat-leaf parsley.

Croque Monsieur

Probably the most popular snack food in France, this hot cheese and ham sandwich can be either pan-fried or broiled.

Makes 2

INGREDIENTS
4 slices white bread
2 tbsp softened butter
2 thin slices lean ham
2 oz Swiss cheese, thinly sliced
1 sprig flat-leaf parsley, to garnish

white bread

Swiss cheese

ham

COOK'S TIP

A flavored butter can be used to complement a sandwich filling – for example, horseradish butter with beef, mustard butter with ham, lemon and dill butter with fish. To make these just beat the chosen flavoring into the softened butter with some seasoning. Other useful flavorings for butter are: anchovy or curry paste, garlic, herbs, Tabasco, or chili. These butters can also be used in open-face sandwiches.

1 Spread the bread with butter.

2 Lay the ham on 2 of the buttered sides of bread.

3 Lay the Swiss cheese slices on top of the ham and sandwich with the buttered bread slices. Press firmly together and cut off the crusts.

4 Spread the top with butter, place on a rack, and cook for 2½ minutes under the broiler preheated to a low to moderate temperature.

5 Turn the sandwiches over, spread the remaining butter over the top, and return to the broiler for 2½ minutes more, until the bread is golden brown and the cheese is beginning to melt. Garnish with a sprig of flat-leaf parsley.

Bruschetta al Pomodoro

Bruschetta is an Italian garlic bread made with the best-quality olive oil you can find and a coarse country bread, or ciabatta. Here, chopped tomatoes are added too.

Makes 2

INGREDIENTS
2 large thick slices coarse country bread
1 large garlic clove
4 tbsp extra-virgin olive oil
2 ripe tomatoes, skinned and chopped
salt and pepper
1 sprig fresh basil, to garnish

country bread

tomatoes

garlic

1 Toast the bread on both sides.

2 Peel the garlic clove and squash with the flat side of a knife blade.

3 Rub the squashed garlic clove over the toast.

4 Drizzle half the olive oil over the toasted bread.

5 Top with the tomatoes, season well, and drizzle over the remaining oil. Place under the broiler to heat through, then garnish with a sprig of basil and eat immediately.

PLAIN BRUSCHETTA

Rub a crushed garlic clove over the toasted bread and drizzle with olive oil.

Pastrami on Rye

Pastrami is wood-smoked brisket of beef that has first been dry-cured in a mixture of garlic, sugar, salt, and spices. This is a kosher sandwich that originated in New York.

Makes 2

INGREDIENTS
2 tbsp softened butter
4 thin slices rye bread
1 tbsp German mustard
¼ lb wafer-thin pastrami
4 dill pickles, sliced lengthwise
radish chrysanthemums and scallion
   tassels, to garnish

rye bread

dill pickles

pastrami

mustard

1 Butter the bread and spread 2 of the slices with a little mustard.

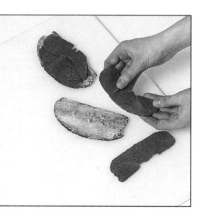

2 Arrange the pastrami slices over the mustard.

3 Top with slices of dill pickle, cover with the remaining bread, and press together firmly. Toast on both sides under a preheated broiler until turning brown. Serve garnished with radish chrysanthemums and scallion tassels.

Fried Mozzarella Sandwich

This sandwich is very popular in southern Italy, where it is known as *Mozzarella in Carrozza*. Be sure to use mozzarella packed in brine for the best flavor. This is also excellent made with Cheddar or Swiss cheese.

Makes 2

INGREDIENTS
¼ lb mozzarella cheese, thickly sliced
4 thick slices white bread, crusts
    removed
salt and pepper
1 egg
2 tbsp milk
oil for shallow-frying

white bread

mozzarella cheese

egg

1 Lay the mozzarella slices on 2 slices of bread, sprinkle with salt and pepper, then top with the remaining bread slices to make 2 cheese sandwiches.

2 Mix the egg and milk together, season, and place in a large shallow dish.

3 Lay the sandwiches in the egg mixture, turn over so that they are saturated and leave there for a few minutes. Pour enough oil into a skillet to give ½ in depth. Heat the oil and fry the sandwich for 3–4 minutes, turning once, until golden brown and crisp. Drain well on paper towels.

VARIATION

Add 2 chopped sun-dried tomatoes or some black olive paste to the sandwich before soaking in egg.

Tostadas with Refried Beans

A tostada is a crisp, fried tortilla used as a base on which to pile the topping of your choice – a variation on a sandwich and a very tasty snack popular on both sides of the border.

Makes 6

INGREDIENTS
2 tbsp oil
1 onion, chopped
2 garlic cloves, chopped
½ tsp chili powder
15 oz can borlotti or pinto beans, drained
⅔ cup chicken stock
1 tbsp tomato paste
2 tbsp chopped fresh cilantro
salt and pepper
6 corn tortillas
3 tbsp Tomato Salsa
2 tbsp sour cream
½ cup grated Cheddar cheese
fresh cilantro leaves, to garnish

beans

onion

tortillas

garlic

chili powder

tomato paste

Cheddar cheese

cilantro

1 Heat the oil in a pan and fry the onion until softened.

2 Add the garlic and chili powder and fry for 1 minute, stirring.

3 Mix in the beans and mash very roughly with a potato masher.

4 Add the stock, tomato paste, chopped cilantro, and seasoning to taste. Mix thoroughly and cook for a few minutes.

5 Fry the tortillas in hot oil for 1 minute, turning once, until crisp, then drain on paper towels.

TOMATO SALSA

Makes about 1¼ cups

1 small onion, chopped
1 garlic clove, crushed
2 fresh green chilies, seeded and
  finely chopped, or 1 tsp bottled
  chopped chilies
1 lb tomatoes, skinned and chopped
salt
2 tbsp chopped fresh cilantro

Stir all the ingredients together until
well mixed.

6 Put a spoonful of refried beans on
each tostada, spoon over some Tomato
Salsa, then some sour cream, sprinkle
with grated Cheddar cheese, and garnish
with cilantro.

Chinese Duck in Pita

This recipe is based on Chinese crispy duck but uses duck breast instead of whole duck. After 15 minutes cooking, the duck breast will still have a pinkish tinge. If you like it well-done, leave it in the oven for about 5 minutes more.

Makes 2

INGREDIENTS
1 duck breast, weighing about 6 oz
3 scallions
3 in piece hothouse cucumber
2 round pita breads
2 tbsp hoi-sin sauce
radish chrysanthemum and scallion tassel, to garnish

pita breads

cucumber

duck breast

hoi-sin sauce

scallions

1 Preheat the oven to 425°F. Skin the duck breast, place the skin and breast separately on a rack, and cook in the oven for 10 minutes.

2 Remove the skin from the oven, cut into pieces, and return to the oven for 5 minutes more.

3 Meanwhile, cut the scallions and cucumber into fine shreds about 1 ½ in long.

4 Heat the pita bread in the oven for a few minutes until puffed up, then split in half to make a pocket.

5 Slice the duck breast thinly.

6 Stuff the duck breast into the pita bread with a little scallion, cucumber, crispy duck skin, and some hoi-sin sauce. Serve garnished with a radish chrysanthemum and scallion tassel.

Tuna Melt

Melts can also be made with a variety of meats such as salami, pastrami, or chicken, then covered with cheese and cooked on a griddle or broiled.

Makes 2

INGREDIENTS
3½ oz can tuna fish, drained and
roughly flaked
2 tbsp mayonnaise
1 tbsp finely chopped celery
1 tbsp finely chopped scallion
1 tbsp chopped fresh parsley
1 tsp lemon juice
2 tbsp softened butter
4 slices whole-wheat bread
2 oz Swiss cheese, sliced
celery leaves and radish roses, to
garnish

whole-wheat bread

scallion

celery

Swiss cheese

tuna fish

parsley

1 Mix together the tuna fish, mayonnaise, celery, scallion, parsley, and lemon juice.

2 Butter the bread slices with half the butter and spread the tuna filling over 2 of them. Cover with cheese slices, then sandwich with the remaining bread.

3 Butter the bread on top and place under a moderate broiler for 1–2 minutes. Turn over, spread with the remaining butter, and broil for 1–2 minutes more, until the cheese begins to melt. Garnish with celery leaves and radish roses.

PASTRAMI MELT

Arrange 2 slices pastrami over a slice of rye bread and spread some mustard on top. Cover with tomato and onion slices, then top with cheese, cover with the buttered bread and broil on both sides.

Reuben Sandwich

A popular delicatessen sandwich that combines rye bread or pumpernickel, corned beef, Swiss cheese, and sauerkraut. The broiled sandwich should be crisp and hot outside, and cold inside.

Makes 2

INGREDIENTS
2 tbsp softened butter
4 slices rye bread or pumpernickel
2 oz wafer-thin corned beef
2 oz Swiss cheese, sliced
1 tbsp tomato ketchup
2 tbsp mayonnaise
6 tbsp sauerkraut
dill pickles and celery leaves, to
    garnish

rye bread

Swiss cheese

sauerkraut

corned beef

1 Butter the pumpernickel and place corned beef on 2 of the slices. Arrange cheese on the other slices.

2 Mix the tomato ketchup and mayonnaise with the sauerkraut.

3 Pile the sauerkraut mixture on top of the cheese and spread to the edges.

4 Lay the other slices, beef side down, on top of the sauerkraut. Butter the bread on top, then broil for 1–2 minutes until crisp. Turn over, butter the second side, and broil for 1–2 minutes more, until the cheese just begins to melt. Serve garnished with dill pickle slices and celery leaves.

VARIATION
Replace the corned beef with pastrami.

Köfte in Pita Pockets

Köfte is the Turkish name for meatballs. These are made with ground lamb and flavored with cumin. Pita bread is also good filled with barbecued or broiled lamb that has been marinated in a little wine and olive oil flavored with garlic, bay, and cumin.

Makes 4

INGREDIENTS
1 slice bread
½ lb ground lamb
1 garlic clove, crushed
1 small onion, finely chopped
1 tsp ground cumin
1 tbsp chopped fresh mint
salt and pepper
1 tbsp pine nuts
flour for coating
oil for shallow-frying
4 pita breads
1 onion, cut into thin rings
2 tomatoes, sliced or cut into wedges

1 Preheat the oven to 425°F. Soak the bread in water for 5 minutes, then squeeze dry and add to the next 7 ingredients. Mix until thoroughly blended and malleable. Shape into small balls the size of a walnut, using dampened hands so that the mixture does not stick. Lightly coat in flour.

2 Shallow-fry for about 6 minutes, turning frequently, until golden brown.

3 Heat the pita bread in the oven for a few minutes until puffed up, then cut a thin strip off one side of each pita to make a pocket.

ground lamb

onion

garlic

cumin

mint

pine nuts

bread

4 Fill with onion rings, tomato wedges, and a few Köfte.

TZATZIKI

Mix together 1½ cups thick Greek-style yogurt, ⅓ cup peeled and grated cucumber, 1 crushed garlic clove, 1 tbsp chopped fresh mint, and seasoning to taste.

LAMB IN PITA POCKETS

Mix together ¼ cup red wine, ¼ cup olive oil, 2 chopped garlic cloves, 1 bay leaf and ½ teaspoon each of ground cumin and ground coriander. Marinate a 6 oz lamb fillet in this mixture for at least 30 minutes. Grill (broil) for 10 minutes, turning once, then slice thinly and stuff into a warmed pita pocket with salad and Tzatziki.

Chili Beef Tacos

These easy-to-prepare sandwiches are now equally at home on both sides of the border. But don't limit yourself to the taco shell, soft flour tortillas are also authentically Mexican.

Makes 4

INGREDIENTS
1 tbsp oil
1 small onion, chopped
2 garlic cloves, chopped
6 oz ground beef
½ tbsp flour
7 oz can tomatoes
½ tbsp finely chopped Jalapeño
    peppers
salt
4 wheat or corn tortillas
3 tbsp sour cream
½ avocado, peeled, pitted and sliced
1 tomato, sliced
Tomato Salsa, to serve (optional)

ground beef

avocado

tortillas

onion

garlic

Jalapeño peppers

1 Heat the oil in a skillet, add the onion, and fry until softened. Add the garlic and beef and cook, stirring so that the meat is broken up as it sears.

2 Stir in the flour, then add the canned tomatoes, peppers, and salt to taste.

3 Heat the tortillas one at a time in a medium-hot lightly oiled pan.

4 Spread a spoonful of the meat mixture over each tortilla.

5 Top each tortilla with some sour cream and avocado and tomato slices. Roll up and eat immediately with Tomato Salsa if liked.

Pizza-topped Biscuits

Use whatever cheese you have on hand – Cheddar, mozzarella, or goat cheese all work well. Add a few olives too, if you like.

Makes 12

Ingredients
6 Cheese and Herb Biscuits
6 tbsp red pesto
2 tomatoes, sliced
1 tsp dried oregano
salt and pepper
2 cups grated Cheddar cheese

Cheese and Herb Biscuits

tomato

Cheddar cheese

oregano

red pesto

1 Cut the biscuits in half, toast on the cut side, and spread with red pesto.

2 Put a slice of tomato on each one and sprinkle with the oregano and seasoning to taste.

3 Pile grated cheese on top of each one and place under a moderate broiler until brown and bubbling.

Cheese and Herb Biscuits

These biscuits are so quick to make, and when cut in half make tasty bases for broiled toppings.

Makes 6

2 cups self-rising flour
1 tsp mustard powder
cayenne pepper
½ tsp salt
4 tbsp margarine
1 tsp dried oregano
¾ cup grated Cheddar cheese
½ cup milk, plus extra to glaze

Preheat the oven to 425°F. Sift the flour, mustard, cayenne, and salt into a mixing bowl and rub in the margarine until the mixture resembles bread crumbs. Mix in the oregano and cheese, then add the milk and mix to a soft dough. Transfer to a floured surface, knead and roll out to a thickness of ½ in. Cut into 3 in rounds with a plain cutter, place on a floured baking sheet, and brush with milk. Bake in the oven for 12–15 minutes until golden. Cool on a wire rack.

Ciabatta Rolls with Goat Cheese

The Tomato Relish gives a piquant bite that nicely complements the goat cheese. If you can't find the rolls, use a ciabatta loaf or country bread instead.

Makes 4

INGREDIENTS
2 ciabatta rolls
4 tbsp Tomato Relish
2 tbsp chopped fresh basil
6 oz goat cheese, thinly sliced
6 black olives, halved and pitted
1 sprig fresh basil, to garnish

ciabatta rolls

Tomato Relish

goat cheese

basil

olives

1 Cut the rolls in half and toast on one side only.

2 Spread a little relish over each half and sprinkle with the chopped basil.

3 Arrange the goat cheese slices on top, then scatter over a few olives. Place under a hot broiler until the goat cheese begins to melt, then serve garnished with a sprig of basil.

TOMATO RELISH

Makes scant 2 cups

3 tbsp olive oil
1 onion, chopped
1 red bell pepper, seeded and
    chopped
2 garlic cloves
¼ tsp chili powder
14 oz can chopped tomatoes
1 tbsp clear honey
2 tsp black olive paste
2 tbsp red-wine vinegar
salt and pepper

Heat the oil and fry the onion and red bell pepper until softened. Add the garlic and the remaining ingredients, and season to taste. Simmer for 15 minutes until thickened.

Ciabatta with Mozzarella and Broiled Onion

Ciabatta is readily available in most supermarkets. It's even more delicious when made with spinach, sun-dried tomatoes, or olives, and you'll probably find these in your local grocery store.

Makes 4

INGREDIENTS
1 ciabatta loaf
4 tbsp red pesto
2 small onions
oil, for brushing
½ lb mozzarella cheese
8 black olives

ciabatta loaf

tomato

onion

mozzarella cheese

olives

red pesto

1 Cut the bread in half horizontally and toast lightly. Spread with the red pesto.

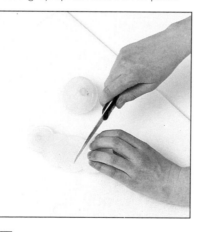

2 Peel the onions and cut horizontally into thick slices. Brush with oil and broil for 3 minutes until lightly browned.

3 Slice the cheese and arrange over the bread. Lay the onion slices on top and scatter some olives over. Cut in half diagonally. Place under a hot broiler for 2–3 minutes until the cheese melts and the onion chars.

Welsh Rarebit

This recipe is traditionally made with English brown ale or red wine, which gives it a delicious flavor. You can use other cheeses too, such as Stilton or Red Leicester. If you put a poached or fried egg on top, the dish becomes a Buck Rarebit.

Makes 4

INGREDIENTS
1 cup grated strong Cheddar cheese
2 tbsp brown ale or beer
1 tsp English mustard
cayenne pepper
4 slices bread

bread

brown ale

mustard

Cheddar cheese

cayenne pepper

1 Put the cheese in a saucepan with the brown ale, mustard, and cayenne pepper, and mix together thoroughly.

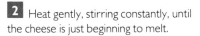

2 Heat gently, stirring constantly, until the cheese is just beginning to melt.

3 Meanwhile, toast the bread. Spread the cheese mixture over the toast.

4 Broil lightly until tinged brown here and there.

Crostini with Tomato and Anchovy

Crostini are little rounds of bread cut from a baguette and toasted or fried, then covered with a savory topping such as melted cheese, olive paste, anchovy, tomato, or chicken liver.

Makes 8

INGREDIENTS
1 small baguette (large enough to give
   8 slices)
2 tbsp olive oil
2 garlic cloves, chopped
4 tomatoes, peeled and chopped
1 tbsp chopped fresh basil
1 tbsp tomato paste
salt and pepper
8 canned anchovy fillets
12 black olives, halved and pitted
1 sprig fresh basil, to garnish

olive oil

baguette

garlic

black olives

basil

anchovy fillets

1 Cut the bread diagonally into 8 slices about ½ in thick and toast until golden on both sides.

CROSTINI WITH ONION AND OLIVE

Fry 2 cups sliced onions in 2 tbsp olive oil until golden brown. Stir in 8 roughly chopped anchovy fillets, 12 halved, pitted black olives, some seasoning, and 1 tsp dried thyme. Spread the toasted bread with 1 tbsp black olive paste and spread a spoonful of the onion mixture over each one.

2 Heat the oil and fry the garlic and tomatoes for 4 minutes. Stir in the basil, tomato paste, and seasoning.

3 Spoon a little tomato mixture on each slice of bread. Place an anchovy fillet on each one and sprinkle with olives. Serve garnished with a sprig of basil.

Focaccia with Hot Artichokes and Olives

Focaccia makes an excellent base for different broiled toppings. Artichoke hearts bottled in oil are best for this.

Makes 3

INGREDIENTS
4 tbsp olive paste or Tapenade
3 Mini Focaccia
1 small red bell pepper, halved and seeded
10 oz bottled or canned artichoke hearts, drained
3 oz pepperoni, sliced
1 tsp dried oregano

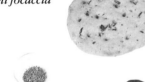
red bell pepper

mini focaccia

oregano

pepperoni

artichoke hearts

1 Preheat the oven to 425°F. Spread the olive paste over the focaccia. Broil the red bell pepper until blackened, put in a plastic bag, seal, and allow to cool for 10 minutes. Skin the pepper and cut into strips.

2 Cut the artichoke hearts in quarters and arrange over the olive paste with the pepperoni.

3 Sprinkle over the red pepper strips and the oregano. Place in the oven for 5–10 minutes until heated through.

OLIVE FOCACCIA

Focaccia is an Italian flat bread made with olive oil and often with olives as well. The amount of water needed varies with the type of flour used, so you may need a little less – or a little more – than the quantity given.

Makes 2 loaves

4 cups bread flour
1 tsp salt
1 tsp dried yeast
pinch of sugar
1 ¼ cups warm water
4 tbsp olive oil
1 cup black olives, pitted and roughly chopped
½ tsp dried oregano

Mix the flour and salt together in a mixing bowl. Put the yeast in a small bowl and mix with half the water and a pinch of sugar to help activate the yeast. Leave for about 10 minutes until dissolved. Add the yeast mixture to the flour along with the oil, olives, and remaining water, and mix to a soft dough, adding a little more water if necessary.

Transfer the dough out to a floured surface and knead for 5 minutes until it is smooth and elastic. Place in a mixing bowl, cover with a damp dish towel and leave in a warm place to rise for about 2 hours or until doubled in size.

Preheat the oven to 425°F. Transfer the dough out to a floured surface and knead again for a few minutes. Divide into 2 portions, then roll out each to a thickness of ½ in in either a round or oblong shape. Place on an oiled baking sheet, using a floured rolling pin to lift the dough. Make indentations all over the surface with your fingertips and sprinkle with the oregano. Bake in the oven for about 15–20 minutes.

FOCACCIA WITH SUN-DRIED TOMATOES AND MOZZARELLA

Spread the focaccia with 3 tbsp chopped sun-dried tomatoes. Slice ½ lb mozzarella cheese and arrange over the top. Sprinkle with 8 pitted and quartered black olives, and heat through in the oven as for the main recipe.

MINI FOCACCIA

Divide the dough into 6 balls. On a floured surface, roll these out to 6 in circles. Finish as for Olive Focaccia, baking for 12–15 minutes.

Pan Bagna

This literally means 'bathed bread' and is basically a Salade Niçoise stuffed into a baguette or roll. The olive oil dressing soaks into the bread when it is left for an hour or so with a weight on top of it.

Makes 4

INGREDIENTS
1 large baguette
⅔ cup French Dressing
1 small onion, thinly sliced
3 tomatoes, sliced
1 small green or red bell pepper, seeded and sliced
2 oz can anchovy fillets, drained
3½ oz can tuna fish, drained
2 oz black olives, halved and pitted

baguette

French Dressing

bell peppers

tomatoes

tuna fish

onion

anchovy fillets

olives

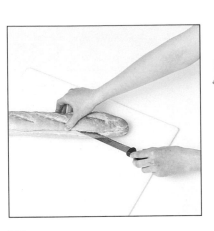

1 Split the baguette horizontally along one side without cutting all the way through the crust.

2 Open the bread out so that it lies flat and sprinkle the French Dressing evenly over the top.

3 Arrange the onion, tomatoes, green or red pepper, anchovies, tuna, and olives on one side of the bread. Close the 2 halves, pressing firmly together.

4 Wrap in plastic wrap, lay a board on top, put a weight on it, and leave for about 1 hour: as well as allowing the dressing to soak into the bread, this makes it easier to eat.

5 Cut the loaf diagonally into 4 equal portions.

FRENCH DRESSING

Olive oil is a must for this dressing; it imparts a rich, fruity flavor, especially if you use that lovely green, virgin olive oil. Make a large quantity at a time and store it in a wine bottle, ready for instant use.

Makes about scant 2 cups

1½ cups extra-virgin olive oil
6 tbsp red-wine vinegar
1 tbsp Moutarde de Meaux
1 garlic clove, crushed
1 tsp clear honey
salt and pepper

Pour the olive oil into a measuring jug and make up to a scant 2 cups with the vinegar. Add the remaining ingredients, then, using a funnel pour into a wine bottle. Put in the cork firmly, give the mixture a thorough shake, and store.

Ciabatta Sandwich

If you can find a ciabatta flavored with sun-dried tomatoes, it improves the flavor of the sandwich. The proscuitto should be sliced very thinly and then cut into strips to make it easier to eat.

Makes 3

INGREDIENTS
4 tbsp mayonnaise
2 tbsp pesto sauce
1 ciabatta loaf
¼ lb provolone or mozzarella cheese, sliced
3 oz prosciutto, cut into strips
4 plum tomatoes, sliced
sprigs fresh basil, torn into pieces

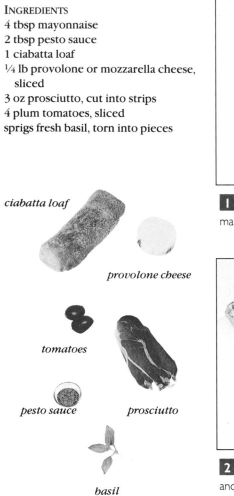

ciabatta loaf

provolone cheese

tomatoes

pesto sauce

prosciutto

basil

1 Thoroughly mix together the mayonnaise and pesto sauce.

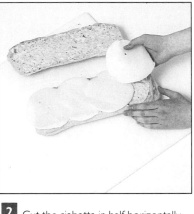

2 Cut the ciabatta in half horizontally and spread the cut side of both halves with the pesto mayonnaise. Lay the cheese over one half of the ciabatta.

3 Cut the prosciutto into strips and arrange over the top. Cover with the sliced tomatoes and torn basil leaves. Sandwich together with the other half and cut into 3 pieces.

Frankfurter and Potato Salad Sandwich

An unlikely mixture to put into a sandwich, but one that works extremely well. If the potato salad is too chunky, chop it a little first. This is best eaten with a knife and fork.

Makes 2

INGREDIENTS
⅔ cup (¼ lb) potato salad
2 scallions, chopped
2 tbsp softened butter
4 slices whole-wheat bread
4 frankfurters
2 tomatoes, sliced

whole-wheat bread

potato salad

tomatoes

scallions

frankfurters

FRANKFURTER AND EGG SALAD SANDWICH

Shell and roughly chop 1 hard-cooked egg and mix with 1 tbsp mayonnaise and 1 tbsp chopped fresh chives. Use in place of the potato salad.

1 Mix the potato salad with the scallions.

2 Butter all 4 slices of bread and divide the potato salad equally between 2 of them, spreading it to the edges.

3 Slice the frankfurters diagonally and arrange over the potato salad with the tomato slices.

4 Sandwich with the remaining bread, press together lightly, and cut in half.

Omelete Roll

An unusual way to serve an omelete but one that
works extremely well, either warm or cold. This is
equally good made with whole-wheat bread, in which
case don't roll the omelete.

Makes 1

INGREDIENTS
1 Cheese and Tomato Roll
2 tsp crushed sun-dried tomatoes
2 eggs
salt and pepper
few sprigs watercress
2 tbsp chopped fresh chives
1 tbsp chopped sun-dried tomatoes
1 tbsp butter

*Cheese and
Tomato Roll*

chives

eggs

sun-dried tomatoes

*crushed sun-
dried tomatoes*

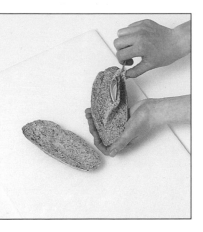

1 Slice the roll horizontally, scoop out some of the crumb to make a hollow, and spread the crushed sun-dried tomato over the bread.

2 Break the eggs into a small bowl, add seasoning, 1 tbsp water, the watercress, chives, and chopped sun-dried tomato, and whisk with a fork.

3 Heat the butter in a small omelete pan until it sizzles.

4 Tip in the egg, then, as it begins to set, draw the sides towards the middle so that more egg touches the hot pan. Repeat this a couple more times.

5 When the egg is just set, lift the edge of the omelete nearest the handle, tilting the pan away from you.

6 Flip the omelete over and gently slip it into the roll.

Salami Hero

This is a huge affair, filled with as much as you can cram into a roll. Fillings vary by region: tuna, egg, cheese, coleslaw, salads, meats, or salami, but there are no hard and fast rules. Fill according to your taste or availability.

Makes 2

INGREDIENTS
2 long crusty rolls
2 tbsp softened butter
few leaves lollo rosso lettuce or
    radicchio
3 oz coleslaw
3 oz Italian salami, sliced
1 tomato, sliced
2 tbsp mayonnaise

lollo rosso lettuce

rolls

tomato

Italian salami

mayonnaise

coleslaw

1 Cut the rolls horizontally three-quarters of the way through, open out sufficiently to take the filling, and butter both cut sides.

2 Arrange lettuce or radicchio leaves on the base, then add a spoonful of coleslaw.

3 Fold the salami slices in half and arrange over the top. Cover with a little more lettuce, tomato slices, and a little mayonnaise. Serve with a napkin!

Classic BLT

This delicious American favorite is made with crispy fried bacon, lettuce, and tomato. Choose the bread you prefer and toast it if you like.

Makes 2

INGREDIENTS
4 slices multi-grain bread
1 tbsp softened butter
8 slices bacon
few crisp lettuce leaves, romaine or
    iceberg
1 large tomato, sliced
2 tbsp mayonnaise

multi-grain bread

tomato

lettuce

bacon

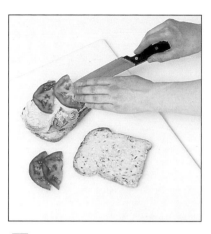

1 Spread 2 of the slices of bread with butter. Lay the lettuce over the bread and cover with sliced tomato.

2 Broil or fry the bacon until it begins to crisp, then arrange it over the sliced tomato.

3 Spread the 2 remaining slices of bread with mayonnaise. Lay over the bacon, press the sandwich together gently, and cut in half.

Roast Beef Triple Decker

This jaw-defying sandwich is made with 3 layers of bread and should be very generously filled. The filling can be varied – chicken, ham, cheese or turkey, with an appropriate spread, like mustard or relish, then a layer of salad and, of course, mayonnaise.

Makes 1

INGREDIENTS
2 tbsp softened butter
2 slices whole-wheat bread
1 slice white or sourdough bread
2 slices rare roast beef
1 tsp Horseradish Relish
few leaves frisée lettuce
1 tomato, sliced
½ avocado, peeled and sliced
2 tbsp mayonnaise
carrot curls and stuffed olives, to
    garnish

bread

tomato

avocado

frisée

roast beef

mayonnaise

1 Butter the whole-wheat bread on one side and the white bread on both sides.

2 Cover one of the brown slices with 2 slices beef, some Horseradish Relish, and then some frisée lettuce.

3 Cover this layer with the white bread, then arrange the tomato and avocado slices on top.

4 Spread mayonnaise over the top, and sandwich with the remaining slice of whole-wheat bread.

5 Press together lightly and cut into quarters.

HORSERADISH RELISH

Makes about ⅓ cup

3 tbsp plain fromage frais
4 tsp grainy mustard
4 tsp prepared horseradish sauce

Mix all ingredients together in a bowl.

6 Put carrot curls and stuffed olives on toothpicks and stick into each sandwich to garnish.

Shrimp, Tomato, and Mayonnaise Sandwich

Use frozen North Atlantic shrimp for the best flavor, and make sure that they are thoroughly thawed and well drained before you assemble the sandwich. Pat them dry with paper towels.

Makes 2

INGREDIENTS
2 tbsp softened butter
1 tsp sun-dried tomato paste
4 slices whole-wheat bread
1 bunch watercress, trimmed
3 tbsp Tomato Mayonnaise
⅔ cup (about ¼ lb) frozen cooked
   peeled shrimp, thawed

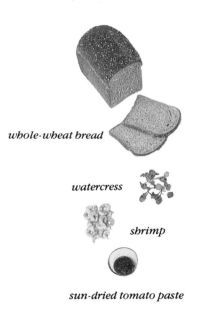

whole-wheat bread

watercress

shrimp

sun-dried tomato paste

1 Mix the butter and tomato paste together until well blended.

2 Spread on the bread and then arrange sprigs of watercress on 2 of the slices.

3 Spread Tomato Mayonnaise all the way to the edges, then divide the shrimp equally over the top. Sandwich together with the remaining bread slices and cut in half or quarters.

TOMATO MAYONNAISE

Makes ¾ cup

Peel, seed, and chop 1 tomato and place in a blender with 1 small crushed garlic clove, 1 tsp brown sugar and 2 tsp tomato paste. Blend and stir into ½ cup mayonnaise.

Chicken and Curry Mayonnaise Sandwich

This is a very useful and appetizing way of using leftover pieces of roast chicken.

Makes 2

INGREDIENTS
4 slices multi-grain bread
2 tbsp softened butter
1 cup sliced cooked chicken
3 tbsp Curry Mayonnaise
1 bunch watercress, trimmed

chicken

multi-grain bread

Curry Mayonnaise

watercress

1 Spread the bread with butter and arrange the chicken over 2 of the slices.

2 Spread Curry Mayonnaise over the chicken slices.

3 Arrange sprigs of watercress on top, cover with the remaining bread, press lightly together, and cut in half.

CURRY MAYONNAISE

Makes about ⅔ cup

½ cup mayonnaise
2 tsp concentrated curry sauce
½ tsp lemon juice
2 tsp strained apricot jam

Mix all the ingredients together thoroughly.

Crab and Avocado Sandwich

The flavors of crab and avocado combine together very successfully to make this a hearty and delicious sandwich.

Makes 4

INGREDIENTS
6 oz canned crab meat in brine,
    drained
2 scallions, chopped
salt and pepper
½ cup mayonnaise
1 large avocado, peeled and halved
1 tbsp lemon juice
4 tbsp softened butter
8 slices multi-grain bread
lettuce leaves, to garnish

mayonnaise

multi-grain bread

avocado

scallions

crab meat

1 Mix the crab meat with the scallions, seasoning, and 2 tbsp of the mayonnaise.

2 Cut the avocado into slices and brush with lemon juice.

3 Butter the bread and divide the crab meat between 4 of the slices, spreading it all the way to the edges.

4 Cover with slices of avocado.

5 Spread the remaining mayonnaise over the top. Cover with the remaining bread slices and press together firmly. Cut off the crusts and cut the sandwiches diagonally into quarters. Garnish with lettuce leaves.

Oriental Chicken Sandwich

This filling is also good served in warmed pita bread, in which case cut the chicken into small cubes before marinating, then broil on skewers and serve warm.

Makes 2

INGREDIENTS
1 tbsp soy sauce
1 tsp clear honey
1 tsp sesame oil
1 garlic clove, crushed
6 oz boneless skinless chicken breast
4 slices white bread
4 tbsp Peanut Sauce
¼ cup bean sprouts
¼ cup red bell pepper, seeded and finely sliced
2 sprigs parsley, to garnish

chicken breast

garlic

bean sprouts

pepper

Peanut Sauce

1 Mix together the soy sauce, honey, sesame oil, and garlic. Brush over the chicken breast.

2 Broil the chicken for 3–4 minutes on each side until cooked through, then slice thinly.

3 Spread 2 slices of the bread with some of the Peanut Sauce.

4 Lay the chicken on the sauce-covered bread.

5 Spread a little more sauce over the chicken.

6 Sprinkle over the bean sprouts and red bell pepper and sandwich together with the remaining slices of bread.

Tuna and Sweet Corn Rolls

Tuna and sweet corn make a delicious combination.
This is a soft filling, so it is better served in a roll,
which is firmer to hold, than between slices of bread.

Makes 2

INGREDIENTS
3½ oz canned tuna, drained and
  flaked
6 tbsp sweet corn kernels
4 tbsp chopped cucumber
2 scallions, chopped
6 tbsp Tartare Sauce
2 multi-grain rolls
2 green or lollo rosso lettuce leaves

sweet corn kernels

lettuce leaves

multi-grain roll

tuna

scallions

Tartare Sauce

cucumber

1 Mix together the tuna, sweet corn,
cucumber, scallions, and 2 tbsp of the
Tartare Sauce.

2 Cut the rolls in half and divide the
filling between each bottom half.

3 Place a lettuce leaf on top, cover with
the remaining Tartare Sauce, and replace
the top of each roll.

TARTARE SAUCE
Mix together 6 tbsp mayonnaise with
2 tsp each of chopped dill pickle,
chopped capers, and chopped parsley.

Bagels and Lox

Bagels were introduced from Germany into the United States with the first Jewish immigrants, but are now popular everywhere. They should be served warm, and the traditional filling is smoked salmon and cream cheese, but other fillings also work well, particularly smoked mackerel.

Makes 2

INGREDIENTS
2 bagels
½ cup (about ¼ lb) cream cheese
1 tsp lemon juice
1 tbsp chopped fresh chives
salt and pepper
a little milk (optional)
¼ lb smoked salmon
dill sprigs and lemon slices, to garnish

bagels

smoked salmon

chives

cream cheese

1 Preheat the oven to 350°F. Wrap the bagels in foil and warm through in the oven for 10 minutes. Mix the cream cheese with the lemon juice, chives, seasoning, and a little milk to thin if necessary.

2 Cut the bagels in half horizontally and spread the bases with the cream cheese.

3 Arrange the smoked salmon over the cream cheese and replace the tops of the bagels.

Farmer's Brunch

A new and tasty twist to a traditional British snack. Use very fresh crusty white bread and top the cheese with a homemade Peach Relish, which goes especially well with Red Leicester cheese.

Makes 2

INGREDIENTS
4 slices crusty white bread
2 tbsp softened butter
¼ lb Red Leicester or Wensleydale cheese (or use Monterey Jack or Tilamook), sliced
3 tbsp Peach Relish
scallions or pickled onions, and tomato wedges, to serve

white bread

Red Leicester

tomato

scallion

Peach Relish

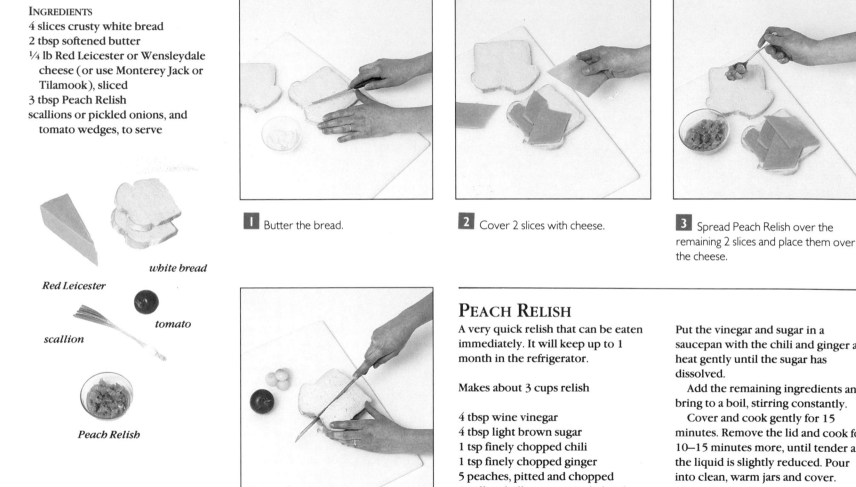

1 Butter the bread.

2 Cover 2 slices with cheese.

3 Spread Peach Relish over the remaining 2 slices and place them over the cheese.

4 Cut in half and serve with scallions or pickled onions, and tomato wedges.

PEACH RELISH

A very quick relish that can be eaten immediately. It will keep up to 1 month in the refrigerator.

Makes about 3 cups relish

4 tbsp wine vinegar
4 tbsp light brown sugar
1 tsp finely chopped chili
1 tsp finely chopped ginger
5 peaches, pitted and chopped
1 yellow bell pepper, seeded and chopped
1 small onion, chopped

Put the vinegar and sugar in a saucepan with the chili and ginger and heat gently until the sugar has dissolved.

Add the remaining ingredients and bring to a boil, stirring constantly.

Cover and cook gently for 15 minutes. Remove the lid and cook for 10–15 minutes more, until tender and the liquid is slightly reduced. Pour into clean, warm jars and cover.

Baguette with Pâté

A lovely picnic sandwich, reminiscent of holidays in France. Fill with pork or duck rillettes, a rich mixture of shredded meat, or a pâté of your choice. It is also delicious filled with Brie or Camembert cheese.

Makes 2

INGREDIENTS
2 demi-baguettes
2 tbsp softened butter
2 tomatoes, sliced
2 in piece cucumber, sliced
few lettuce leaves
¼ lb Country Pâté or pork rillettes

baguettes

Country Pâté

cucumber

tomatoes

1 Cut the baguettes three-quarters of the way through horizontally and spread the cut sides with butter.

2 Fill with a layer of tomato and cucumber slices.

3 Lay the lettuce leaves over the top.

4 Spoon half the rillettes or pâté into each baguette and press together firmly.

COUNTRY PÂTÉ

Makes about 2 lb

½ lb bacon slices, rind removed
12 oz ground pork
½ lb pork liver, ground
¼ lb pork sausagemeat
1 onion, finely chopped
2 garlic cloves, crushed
1 tsp chopped fresh thyme
1 tbsp chopped fresh parsley
salt and pepper

Preheat the oven to 325°F. Stretch the bacon with a metal spatula and use three-quarters of it to line a 3¾ cup terrine mold. Set the remaining bacon aside.

Put the rest of the ingredients in a bowl and mix together thoroughly, or combine them in a food processor. Transfer to the terrine mold and smooth the top evenly. Cover with the remaining bacon.

Cover with a lid, or foil, and place in a roasting pan half-filled with water and cook in the oven for 1¼–1½ hours.

Remove the lid or foil, cover with baking paper, place a 2¼ lb weight on top and leave until cold.

BRIE AND TOMATO BAGUETTE

Put a little lettuce and a few tomato slices in the baguette, then top with 2 oz ripe Brie slices and a few halved and pitted black olives.

Herring and Apple on Rye

You can use rollmops, herrings in wine sauce or any other pickled herrings you like.

Makes 4

INGREDIENTS
2 tbsp softened butter
4 slices rye bread
few lettuce leaves
4 pickled herring fillets
1 red apple, cored and sliced
1 tsp lemon juice
4 tbsp Fennel and Sour Cream
    Dressing
fennel sprigs, to garnish

rye bread

lettuce

apples

pickled herring

fennel

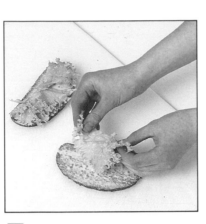

1 Spread the butter on the bread and cover with a few lettuce leaves.

2 Cut the herring fillets in half and arrange on top.

3 Brush the apple slices with lemon juice and arrange around the herring.

4 Spoon over some Fennel and Sour Cream Dressing and garnish with fennel.

HERRING, POTATO, AND DILL PICKLE

Put 1 tbsp potato salad on a lettuce leaf, arrange a herring fillet on top and garnish with sliced dill pickle and cherry tomatoes. Top with a fennel sprig.

BEET, HERRING, AND ONION

Put some sliced, cooked beet over the lettuce, arrange a herring fillet on top, and garnish with thinly sliced onion rings, Fennel and Sour Cream Dressing, and a fennel sprig.

Ham and Asparagus on Rye

Be creative in your arrangement of the ingredients here. You could make ham cornets, or wrap the asparagus in the ham, or use different meats such as salami, mortadella, or Black Forest ham.

Makes 4

INGREDIENTS
12 asparagus spears
½ cups (about ¼ lb) cream cheese
4 slices rye bread
4 slices ham
few leaves frisée lettuce
2 tbsp mayonnaise
4 radish roses, to garnish

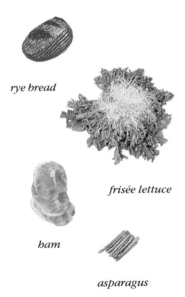

rye bread

frisée lettuce

ham

asparagus

1 Cook the asparagus until tender, drain, pat dry with paper towels, and cool.

2 Spread cream cheese over the rye bread and arrange the ham in folds over the top.

3 Lay 3 asparagus spears on each sandwich.

4 Arrange the lettuce on top of the spears and spoon over some mayonnaise.

5 Garnish with radish roses and serve extra mayonnaise separately in a small bowl if liked.

SALAMI AND COTTAGE CHEESE ON RYE

Omit the asparagus. Arrange 3 salami slices on top with a spoonful of cottage cheese and chopped fresh chives. Garnish with watercress, chives, and chive flowers.

Scrambled Egg and Tomato Fingers

Pumpernickel makes a good firm base for these finger sandwiches and its flavor combines especially well with that of scrambled egg.

Makes 6

INGREDIENTS
2 tbsp softened butter
2 slices pumpernickel bread
2 eggs
1 tbsp milk
salt and pepper
1 tbsp light cream
2 tbsp chopped fresh chives
small fresh sprouts
3 canned anchovy fillets, halved
2 sun-dried tomatoes, cut into strips
tomato rose and scallion tassel, to
    garnish

pumpernickel bread

eggs   *anchovy fillets*

small fresh sprouts

sun-dried tomatoes

1 Butter the pumpernickel and cut into 6 fingers.

2 Whisk the eggs lightly with the milk and add seasoning to taste. Cook the eggs in a little melted butter over a gentle heat, stirring constantly until lightly scrambled.

3 Stir in the cream and chives, and leave to cool.

4 Arrange some sprouts at the ends of the pumpernickel fingers and spoon over the egg. Place the anchovies and sun-dried tomato strips on top of the egg. Garnish with a tomato rose and scallion tassel.

Smoked Salmon and Gravlax Sauce

Gravlax is cured fresh salmon: it is marinated in dill, salt, and sugar and left for 2–3 days with weights on top. It can be bought now in many supermarkets and you can use it instead of smoked salmon if you wish.

Makes 8

INGREDIENTS
2 tbsp softened butter
1 tsp grated lemon zest
4 slices rye or pumpernickel bread
¼ lb smoked salmon
few leaves frisée lettuce
lemon slices
cucumber slices
4 tbsp Gravlax Sauce
dill sprigs, to garnish

frisée lettuce

cucumber

lemon

smoked salmon

rye bread　　*dill*

1 Mix the butter and lemon zest together, spread over the bread, and cut in half diagonally.

2 Arrange the smoked salmon over the top to cover.

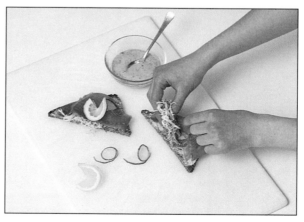

3 Add a little frisée lettuce and a lemon or cucumber slice. Spoon over some Gravlax Sauce, then garnish with dill.

Tapenade and Quails' Eggs

Tapenade, a purée made from capers, olives, and anchovies, is an excellent partner to eggs. Of course you can use ordinary eggs, but quails' eggs look very pretty on open-face sandwiches.

Makes 8

INGREDIENTS
8 quails' eggs
1 small baguette
3 tbsp Tapenade
few leaves frisée lettuce
3 small tomatoes, sliced
4 canned anchovy fillets, halved
   lengthways
black olives
parsley sprigs, to garnish

baguette

frisée lettuce

Tapenade

tomatoes

quails' eggs

1 Boil the quails' eggs for 5 minutes, then plunge straight into cold water to cool. Crack the shells and remove them very carefully.

2 Cut the baguette into diagonal slices and spread with some Tapenade.

3 Arrange the lettuce and tomato slices on top.

4 Halve the quails' eggs and place over the tomato.

5 Finish with a little more Tapenade, the anchovies, and olives. Garnish with small parsley sprigs.

TAPENADE

Makes 1¼ cups

Put a 3½ oz can drained tuna in a food processor with 1½ tbsp capers, 10 canned anchovy fillets, and ¾ cup pitted black olives and blend until smooth, scraping down the sides as necessary. Gradually add 4 tbsp olive oil through the feeder tube and mix well.

Roquefort and Pear Brioche

Roquefort is delicious served with pear, but other blue cheeses, such as Stilton or Cambozola, can be used instead. Toasted brioche makes a good base but must be eaten immediately as it quickly becomes soft once filled.

Makes 4

INGREDIENTS
4 slices brioche loaf
½ cup cottage cheese
few sprigs arugula
¼ lb Roquefort cheese, sliced
1 ripe pear, quartered, cored and
    sliced
juice of ½ lemon
4 pecans, to garnish
viola flowers, to garnish (optional)

cottage cheese

pears

arugula

pecans

Roquefort cheese

1 Toast the brioche and spread with the cottage cheese.

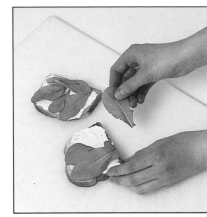

2 Arrange the arugula leaves on top of the cheese.

3 Place the sliced Roquefort on top.

4 Brush the pear slices with lemon juice to prevent discoloration.

5 Arrange the pear slices, overlapping, in a fan shape on the cheese.

6 Garnish with pecans (whole or chopped) and a viola flower if you wish.

PARTY SANDWICHES

Sandwich Train

This is a simple way to make sandwiches more appealing to small children, who can sometimes be difficult to please.

Makes 2 trains

INGREDIENTS
2 sandwiches made with soft filling, such as cream cheese or spread
cucumber peel, cut into narrow strips
radishes
a little sandwich filling
1 celery stick
1 carrot
1 cooked beet
cream cheese, lettuce, and pretzel stick, to garnish (optional)

bread

radishes

beet

carrot

celery

cucumber

1 Remove the crusts from the sandwiches and cut each one into 4 squares.

2 Cut the squares in half again to make 8 small sandwiches.

3 Make an engine using 3 of the sandwiches. Arrange the remaining sandwiches behind the engine, placing cucumber strips to resemble tracks.

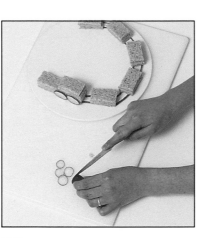

4 Slice the radishes and stick on to the sides of the train with a little sandwich filling to resemble wheels.

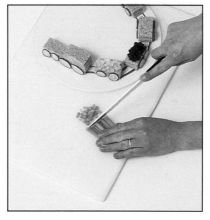

5 Dice the celery, carrot, and beet and pile onto the freight cars to resemble cargo.

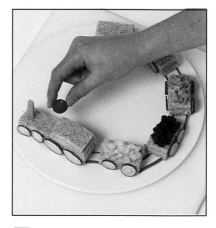

6 Cut a carrot funnel, top with cream cheese smoke if liked, and place on the engine with half a radish. If you want to make a tree, tie some lettuce on to a pretzel stick and stick it in position with a blob of cream cheese.

Log Cabin

This takes a little time but is a great favorite with children.

Makes 1

INGREDIENTS
4 sandwiches made with chosen
filling, crusts removed
pretzel sticks
¼ cup cottage cheese
1 tomato
1 carrot
1 radish
1 in piece cucumber

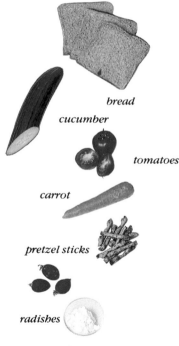

bread

cucumber

tomatoes

carrot

pretzel sticks

radishes

cottage cheese

1 Place 2 of the sandwich rounds on a board and cut each into small rectangular sandwiches.

2 Cut each of the remaining 2 sandwich rounds into 4 triangles.

3 Stack the rectangular sandwiches together to form the cabin and place 6 of the triangles on top to form the roof. (Serve the rest of the triangles separately.)

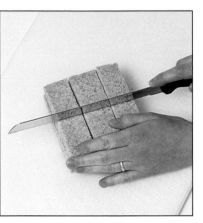

4 Arrange pretzel sticks on the roof to look like logs, sticking with a little cottage cheese or sandwich filling if necessary.

5 Break the remaining pretzel sticks into 1 in lengths and use to make a fence around the cabin, sticking in position with cottage cheese.

6 Cut the tomatoes into doors and windows. Cut the carrot into a chimney, attach it using cottage cheese, and add some cottage cheese smoke. Cut flowers from radishes and carrots. Dice the cucumber finely and arrange on the plate to resemble a path.

Sailing Sandwich

A novelty shape may tempt even the most awkward child. The basic sandwich shape is quick and easy to make, though it's a bit more time consuming to add the trimmings.

Makes 1

INGREDIENTS
1 sandwich made with chosen filling
butter
chopped fresh parsley
few pretzel sticks
paprika
shredded lettuce
tomato ketchup and small pieces of
    lemon rind and cucumber, to
    garnish (optional)

lettuce

bread

pretzel sticks

1 Remove the crusts from the sandwich and cut 2 triangular sails from it. Shape the remaining piece of sandwich to resemble a boat.

2 Spread the long edges of the sails with a little butter and dip in chopped parsley.

3 Turn one sail over and arrange 2 sides together with the pretzel sticks in the center to represent the mast.

4 Spread the boat shape with butter, dip into paprika, and place below the sails. Arrange shredded lettuce underneath to represent the sea. If liked, you can pipe a number on the sail with tomato ketchup. Cut out a sun from lemon rind and a flag from cucumber.

Sailing Ships

A novelty sandwich that you can prepare with different fillings. The processed cheese slices make wonderful sails.

Makes 12

INGREDIENTS
6 small rolls
½ lb chosen filling
chopped fresh parsley
2 tomatoes, quartered and seeded
2 radishes
6 processed cheese slices

small rolls

tomatoes

cheese slices

chives

1 Cut each roll in half horizontally and trim the base so that it stands evenly. Put 1 tbsp of the filling onto each half and spread to the edges, mounding it slightly. Surround the filling with a border of chopped parsley if you like.

2 Cut the tomatoes into thin strips and arrange around the edge of each half-roll.

3 Cut the radishes into strips and 2 triangles. Cut the cheese into sail shapes. Thread each sail onto a toothpick and stand in the filling, supporting it with radish strips if necessary.

PEANUT FILLING

Mix together 3 tbsp crunchy peanut butter and 3 tbsp tomato chutney.

CHEESE AND PINEAPPLE FILLING

Thoroughly combine ½ cup cottage cheese, 2 tbsp drained and chopped canned pineapple, and add seasoning to taste.

Wigwams

Choose a square-shaped loaf, either brown or white, so that you can cut even-sized triangles; the bread should also be thinly sliced.

Makes 4

INGREDIENTS
4 sandwiches, made with chosen
  filling
butter
chopped fresh parsley
small sprouts or flat-leaf parsley
shredded lettuce
1 red bell pepper (optional)
pretzel sticks (optional)

flat-leaf parsley

bell pepper

bread

lettuce

small sprouts

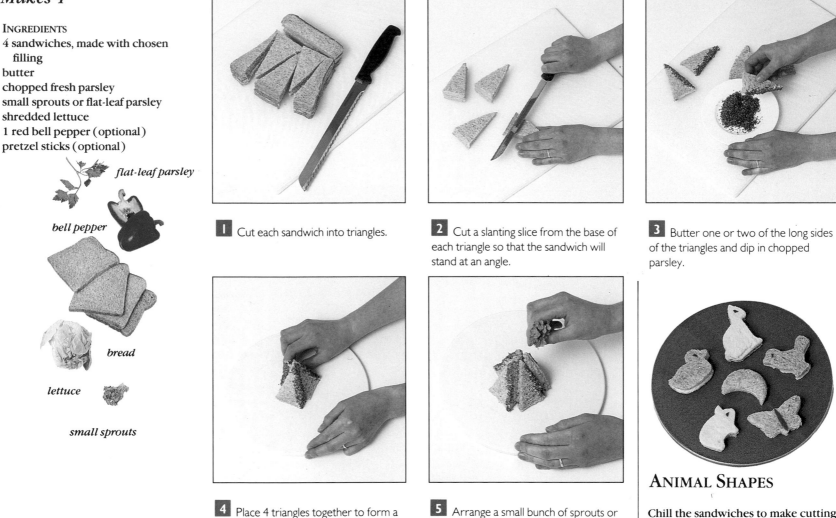

1 Cut each sandwich into triangles.

2 Cut a slanting slice from the base of each triangle so that the sandwich will stand at an angle.

3 Butter one or two of the long sides of the triangles and dip in chopped parsley.

4 Place 4 triangles together to form a wigwam shape.

5 Arrange a small bunch of sprouts or flat-leaf parsley to fit in between the sandwiches at the top. Around the base of the wigwam, arrange shredded lettuce and, if liked, strips of red bell pepper cut zig-zag fashion along one edge. Pretzel sticks may be used to represent poles.

ANIMAL SHAPES

Chill the sandwiches to make cutting easier. Use shaped cutters to make animals, stars, crescents, or hearts as liked. Put a piece of radish on each sandwich to represent an eye or, in the case of a butterfly, a body.

Smoked Salmon Pinwheels

Use a small, fresh, unsliced loaf for these so that you can cut the bread lengthwise and achieve a reasonable-sized pinwheel. The bread is easier to slice if it is half-frozen.

Makes 56

INGREDIENTS
1 small unsliced whole-wheat loaf
1 small lemon
6 tbsp softened butter
1 tbsp chopped fresh dill
½ lb smoked salmon slices
black pepper

lemons

whole-wheat bread

smoked salmon

dill

1 Slice the loaf carefully along its length into 8 thin slices. Cut off the crusts.

2 Grate the lemon zest finely and mix together with the butter and dill.

3 Spread on each slice and arrange smoked salmon over the bread to cover, leaving a strip of buttered bread at one short end. Grind some black pepper over the top.

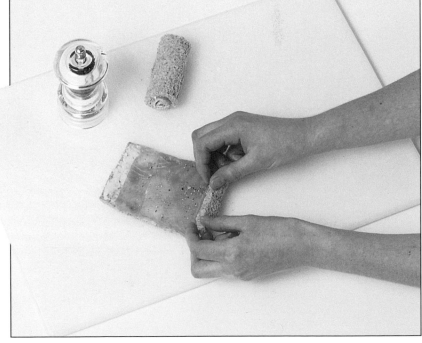

4 With the salmon-covered short end towards you, roll up the bread carefully and tightly, like a jelly roll. The buttered end will ensure the bread sticks together.

5 Wrap in plastic wrap and chill for
1 hour. This will help the filling and bread
to set in the rolled position and ensure
that it does not unwind on slicing. Repeat
with the remaining slices.

6 Using a sharp knife, cut each roll into
½ in slices.

Asparagus Rolls

Use green asparagus as it is usually thinner and looks more attractive. A 12 oz can usually contains about 20 spears.

Makes 20

INGREDIENTS
20 slices whole-wheat bread, crusts
  removed
½ cup softened butter
salt and pepper
12 oz can asparagus tips, drained
lemon slices and fresh edible flowers,
  to garnish

black pepper

whole-wheat bread

asparagus

butter

1 Roll the bread lightly with a rolling pin (this makes it easier to roll up without cracking). Mix the butter and seasoning and spread over each slice of bread.

2 Lay an asparagus tip at one end of the bread with the tip overlapping slightly. Roll up tightly, like a jelly roll, and press the end so that the butter sticks it together.

3 Pack the rolls tightly together, wrap in plastic wrap and chill for 1 hour so that they set in a rolled position and do not unwind when served. Serve garnished with lemon slices and fresh flowers if liked.

Striped Sandwiches

These are fragile when cut, so be sure to chill them for a couple of hours before slicing. To achieve a more contrasting effect, you may like to add a little green food coloring to the Cheese and Chive Filling.

Makes 32

INGREDIENTS
6 slices brown bread
4 slices white bread
1 quantity Tuna and Tomato Filling
½ quantity Egg and Sprout Filling
½ quantity Cheese and Chive Filling
cucumber slices, chives, and fresh
    flowers, to garnish

bread

*Cheese and
Chive Filling*

*Egg and
Sprout Filling*

*Tuna and
Tomato Filling*

1 Start with a slice of brown bread and spread it with Tuna and Tomato Filling.

2 Place a white slice on top and spread with Egg and Sprout Filling. Repeat with Cheese and Chive Filling, then the tuna again, using brown and white bread alternately. Repeat with the remaining fillings and bread. Wrap in foil and chill for 2 hours.

3 Unwrap, cut off the crusts and, using a sharp knife, cut into ½ in slices. Cut the slices in half and serve garnished with cucumber slices, chives, and fresh flowers if liked.

Sandwich Horns

These are good sandwiches for a party, but avoid using dry fillings. Smooth soft fillings, such as cream cheese, pâté, or taramasalata, are most suitable. Use thinly sliced bread to make the shaping easier.

Makes 8

INGREDIENTS
8 thin slices bread
½ cup cottage cheese
1 tbsp mixed chopped fresh parsley, chives, and thyme
salt and pepper
½ cup each Avocado Filling and Cream Cheese Filling
few sprigs fresh herbs, to garnish

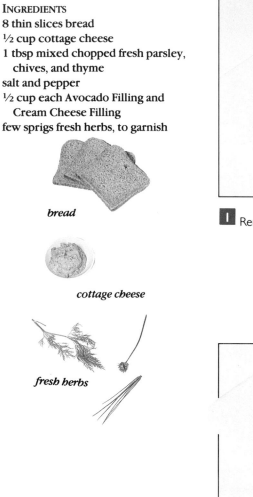

bread

cottage cheese

fresh herbs

1 Remove the crusts from the bread.

2 Cut one corner off each slice, rounding it slightly. For small horns cut a smaller square of bread.

3 Mix the cottage cheese and chopped herbs together with some seasoning. Spread the bread with about half of this mixture.

4 Lift the two sides and fold one over the other with the rounded area at the base of the horn. Stick the bread in position with the Cheese Filling. Secure with a toothpick and chill for 20 minutes to firm up. Repeat with the Avocado Filling and Smoked Salmon Filling.

5 Hold the horn upright in one hand and spoon in the remaining filling.

SMOKED SALMON FILLING

Put 2 oz smoked salmon pieces in a blender with 5 tbsp heavy cream, 1 tsp lemon juice, and a little black pepper. Blend briefly – not too much or the cream will curdle. The result should be a rough purée.

6 Remove the toothpick before serving and garnish with a sprig of herbs.

Cucumber Sandwiches

These traditional afternoon-tea sandwiches are easy to prepare and always popular.

Makes 4

INGREDIENTS
½ cucumber
2 tbsp white-wine vinegar
4 tbsp softened butter
8 slices white bread
salt and pepper

bread

white-wine vinegar

cucumber

butter

1 Cut a few thin slices of cucumber to use as a garnish and set aside, then peel the rest and slice thinly. Place in a bowl, pour over the vinegar, and leave to marinate for 30 minutes. Drain well.

2 Butter the bread, arrange the cucumber slices over half the slices, and sprinkle with salt and pepper.

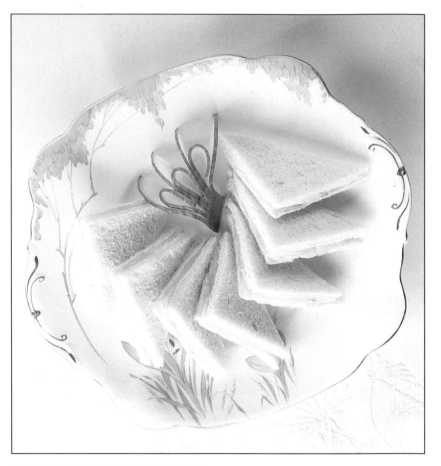

WATERCRESS SANDWICHES

Finely chop 1 bunch watercress. Spread 4 tbsp mayonnaise over 8 slices buttered whole-wheat bread. Arrange the watercress over 4 of the slices, season well, and sandwich together with the remaining 4 slices.

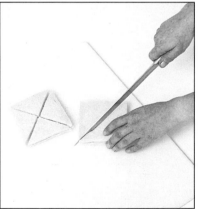

3 Cover with the remaining buttered bread to make 4 sandwiches. Press together firmly and cut off the crusts. Cut each sandwich into 4 triangles and serve garnished with the cucumber slices.

Spicy Chicken Canapés

These tiny little cocktail sandwiches have a spicy filling, finished with different toppings. Use square bread so that you can cut more rounds and have less wastage from each sandwich.

Makes 18

INGREDIENTS

⅓ cup finely chopped cooked
   chicken
2 scallions, finely chopped
2 tbsp chopped red bell pepper
6 tbsp Curry Mayonnaise
6 slices white bread
1 tbsp paprika
1 tbsp chopped fresh parsley
2 tbsp chopped salted peanuts

bell pepper

bread

parsley

cooked chicken

scallions

Curry Mayonnaise

1 Mix the chicken with the chopped scallions, red bell pepper, and half the Curry Mayonnaise.

2 Spread the mixture over 3 of the bread slices and sandwich with the remaining bread, pressing well together. Spread the remaining Curry Mayonnaise over the top and cut into 1½ in circles using a plain cutter.

3 Dip into paprika, chopped parsley or chopped nuts, and arrange on a plate.

INDEX